WORI

For

The Awe of God

The Astounding Way a Healthy Fear of God Transforms Your Life

(Practical Exercises for Implementing of John Bevere's Book)

Life Reads

Please note that this Companion Workbook is designed to complement the original book, not to serve as a replacement. Its purpose is to further enrich and deepen the reader's understanding of the concepts presented in the original book.

Contents

How To Use This Workbook

This workbook has been thoughtfully designed to enhance your understanding of the original book and help you apply its teachings in a practical way. To begin, we recommend starting with the "Summary of the Original Book" at the beginning of the workbook. This concise overview will refresh your memory on the main ideas and concepts presented in the source material, ensuring you have a solid foundation to build upon.

As you delve into each chapter, you will find "Key Lessons" and "Self-Reflection Questions." These sections are designed to help you dive deeper into the core principles and apply them to your life. The "Key Lessons" provide a distilled version of the central idea's main takeaways, while the "Self-Reflection Questions" offer actionable steps to put these lessons into practice. We encourage you to engage actively with these Questions, reflecting on your own experiences and goals as you work through each chapter.

This workbook not only encourages self-reflection but also provides a set of hands-on implementation exercises. These exercises are thoughtfully designed to serve as practical applications of the concepts introduced in the book. Each exercise is meticulously crafted to lead you through a transformative journey, empowering you to actively integrate these ideas into your daily life. By participating in these exercises, you will acquire firsthand experience and foster the development of fresh habits, attitudes, and perspectives.

Finally, towards the end of the workbook, you will discover the "Self-Assessment Questions." This section is a valuable opportunity for self-reflection and evaluation. Use these questions to assess your understanding of the book's content and gauge your progress in applying the principles outlined in the original text.

Throughout your journey with this workbook, keep in mind that the true value lies in your commitment to self-improvement and personal growth. Embrace the exercises, take notes, and be open to exploring new perspectives and ideas. By actively participating in this workbook, you will not only deepen your comprehension of the original book but also unlock the potential for meaningful transformation in your life. Get ready to embark on a rewarding journey of self-discovery and growth!

Summary

"The Awe of God: The Astounding Way a Healthy Fear of God Transforms Your Life" by John Bevere is a thought-provoking and spiritually enriching book that delves into the concept of fearing God in a positive and transformative manner. In this illuminating work, Bevere explores the notion of awe and reverence for the divine and how it can profoundly impact one's life and faith journey.

The book begins by laying a strong foundation, explaining the difference between a healthy fear of God and an unhealthy one. The author emphasizes that the fear of God is not about being afraid of punishment but rather recognizing the majesty, power, and sovereignty of God. Bevere presents a compelling argument that a proper reverence for God can bring about a deep and intimate connection with Him, transforming one's relationship with the divine from a legalistic one to a loving and awe-inspired communion.

Bevere delves into the Scriptures to support his assertions, drawing from both the Old and New Testaments to illustrate the principles of a healthy fear of God. He unpacks the wisdom found in Proverbs, the experiences of various biblical figures, and the teachings of Jesus to elucidate how the awe of God plays a pivotal role in a believer's journey. These scriptural references are skillfully interwoven with personal anecdotes, making the book relatable and engaging.

Furthermore, the author explores the practical implications of fearing God, demonstrating how it impacts areas such as personal morality, decision-making, relationships, and even one's destiny. He encourages readers to cultivate a lifestyle of awe and reverence, highlighting the transformative potential it holds for every aspect of their lives. Bevere provides a step-by-step guide for developing and nurturing a healthy fear of God, making this book an invaluable resource for those seeking a deeper, more meaningful spiritual connection.

In the concluding sections of the book, John Bevere addresses the rewards of living with the awe of God as a guiding principle, emphasizing the eternal significance of such a perspective. He reiterates that a proper fear of God leads to a life of wisdom, blessing, and an unshakable faith. "The Awe of God" is a compelling work that challenges readers to reevaluate their understanding of God and encourages them to embrace a transformative and awe-inspired journey of faith. It is an insightful and inspirational guide that offers practical wisdom for those seeking to deepen their relationship with the divine and experience the profound impact of the awe of God in their lives.

CENTRAL IDEA 1
Embracing Fear of God

Key Lessons

1. Reframing Fear of God: The "fear of God" should not be viewed in the conventional sense of fear as something negative. Instead, it's about understanding that this fear can inspire reverence, awe, and a deep, intimate relationship with the divine. It's a unique type of fear that can lead to personal and spiritual growth.

2. Constructive Fear vs. Destructive Fear: The distinction between constructive fear and destructive fear is essential. Constructive fear encourages positive change by instilling reverence for a higher power, helping individuals develop a strong moral compass, and guiding their actions and decisions. Destructive fear, on the other hand, stifles progress and leads to anxiety, often causing people to avoid challenges and opportunities for personal growth.

3. Transformation and Empowerment: Fearing God in the right way can lead to personal transformation and empowerment. Individuals who embrace this concept often find meaning and purpose in their lives, and it can help them turn their lives around by fostering genuine respect for the divine.

4. Avoiding Pitfalls: Recognizing the difference between constructive and destructive fear in various life contexts is crucial. This awareness can help individuals avoid unnecessary pitfalls and make better decisions. It encourages them to confront challenges and growth opportunities rather than shrinking away from them due to fear.

5. Positive Traits and Fulfillment: Embracing constructive fear can lead to the development of lasting positive traits such as self-awareness, wisdom, and emotional intelligence. Ultimately, it can contribute to living a fulfilling life where individuals are guided by their reverence for a higher power and their moral compass.

Self-Reflection Questions

How do you personally interpret the concept of "fearing God" or a higher power, and how has this interpretation evolved over time?

_____

_____

_____

_____

_____

_____

_____

_____

_____

_____

In your own life, can you recall moments when constructive fear has motivated you to make positive changes or develop a stronger moral compass? What were the results of those experiences?

_____

_____

_____

_____

_____

_____

_____

_____

_____

_____

_____

_____

Have you ever been held back by destructive fear, causing you to avoid taking risks or pursuing your dreams? How did this fear impact your life, and what lessons did you learn from it?

_____

_____

_____

_____

_____

_____

_____

_____

_____

_____

_____

Reflect on your current relationship with the divine or any higher power you believe in. How does this relationship influence your sense of reverence, awe, and purpose in life?

_____

_____

_____

_____

_____

_____

_____

_____

_____

_____

_____

How can you apply the distinction between constructive and destructive fear to your daily life and decision-making to promote personal and spiritual growth?

_____

_____

_____

_____

_____

_____

_____

_____

_____

_____

_____

CENTRAL IDEA 2

Fear Transcended: Cultivating Reverence.

Key Lessons

1. Reverence Inspires Connection: Reverence for a higher power or a greater purpose encourages individuals to recognize that they are part of something more significant than themselves. This recognition inspires a sense of connection and interdependence with the world around them.

2. Positive Contribution to Communities: When individuals view themselves as part of a vast, interconnected web, they are more inclined to contribute positively to their communities and the world. This perspective can lead to acts of kindness and service, benefiting not only the individual but also society as a whole.

3. Transformative Power of Reverence: Many people who initially struggle in life find solace and purpose through reverence for a higher power. Their stories demonstrate how reverence can be transformative, inspiring positive change within themselves and becoming a beacon of hope for others facing similar challenges.

4. Development of a Moral Compass: Reverence encourages individuals to live according to their deepest values and principles, fostering the development of a solid moral compass. This integrity strengthens their connection to the divine and paves the way for personal growth, resilience, and a sense of purpose.

5. Psychological Benefits: Research has shown that cultivating reverence can have tangible psychological benefits. People who revere a higher power often experience increased feelings of gratitude, happiness, and inner peace. These positive emotions can enhance mental health and overall well-being, providing a strong foundation for personal growth and transformation.

Self-Reflection Questions

How do you personally define reverence, and what role does it play in your life? Are there specific ways you demonstrate reverence for something greater than yourself?

_____

_____

_____

_____

_____

_____

_____

_____

_____

_____

_____

_____

In what ways do you view yourself as part of a larger interconnected web, and how does this perspective influence your actions and contributions to your community and the world?

_____

_____

_____

_____

_____

_____

_____

_____

_____

_____

_____

Have you experienced moments of personal transformation or witnessed others who found solace and purpose through reverence for a higher power? How has this impacted your beliefs about the power of reverence to inspire positive change?

_____

_____

_____

_____

_____

_____

_____

_____

_____

_____

_____

_____

How does your moral compass align with your deepest values and principles, and in what ways does acting with integrity strengthen your connection to the divine? How has this connection empowered you in facing life's challenges?

_____

_____

_____

_____

_____

_____

_____

_____

_____

_____

_____

_____

Have you personally experienced the psychological benefits of cultivating reverence, such as increased feelings of gratitude, happiness, and inner peace? How have these positive emotions impacted your mental health and overall well-being, and how do they contribute to your personal growth and transformation?

_____

_____

_____

_____

_____

_____

_____

_____

_____

_____

_____

_____

CENTRAL IDEA 3

The Fear-Humility Connection.

Key Lessons

1. Humility and a Constructive Fear of God: Embrace a humble perspective and a constructive fear of a higher power to stay grounded and aware of your limitations. This can lead to a deeper connection with yourself, others, and the divine, fostering personal growth and meaningful relationships.

2. Learn from a Multi-Billionaire's Journey: Take inspiration from individuals who have achieved success by humbly relying on divine guidance and accepting failures as part of their journey. Embrace the process and trust in it, even when things don't make sense, to achieve career and networking success.

3. Effective Listening and Learning: Approach conversations with a willingness to understand and appreciate different perspectives. Recognize that you don't have all the answers, and by doing so, you open yourself up to the wisdom and insights of those around you.

4. Empathy and Compassion: A humble mindset makes you more empathetic and compassionate, allowing

you to recognize our shared humanity and interconnectedness. This approach to others fosters kind understanding and strengthens connections between people and communities.

5. Humility for a Happy Life: Understand that humility is not just a virtue but a crucial component of a happy and fulfilled life. It helps maintain balance, promotes personal growth, meaningful relationships, and creates a positive and empathetic environment that contributes to long-term happiness and well-being.

Self-Reflection Questions

How do you currently view the role of humility in your life
and decision-making processes?

_____

_____

_____

_____

_____

_____

_____

_____

_____

_____

_____

Are you open to the idea of seeking divine guidance or trusting a higher power in your journey, even in times of uncertainty?

_____

_____

_____

_____

_____

_____

_____

_____

_____

_____

_____

In your interactions with others, do you genuinely approach conversations with a willingness to understand and appreciate different perspectives, or is there room for improvement?

_____

_____

_____

_____

_____

_____

_____

_____

_____

_____

_____

Have you embraced a mindset of humility that fosters empathy and compassion in your daily interactions with people, or do you find yourself struggling to recognize our shared humanity?

_____

_____

_____

_____

_____

_____

_____

_____

_____

_____

_____

What steps can you take to further cultivate humility in your life and strengthen the connections you have with both yourself and those around you?

_____

_____

_____

_____

_____

_____

_____

_____

_____

_____

_____

_____

CENTRAL IDEA 4
The Path to Wisdom

Key Lessons

1. Constructive Fear Promotes Self-Awareness: The fear of God, when approached constructively, encourages individuals to reflect on their actions, acknowledge their limitations, and seek guidance from a higher power. This self-awareness is the foundation for personal growth and wisdom.

2. The Transformative Power of Faith: The example of Max Jukes and Jonathan Edwards demonstrates the impact of faith and holy fear on family legacies. Jonathan Edwards and his wife's strong foundation of faith elevated their lives and those of their descendants, illustrating how faith can lead to positive outcomes and wisdom.

3. Deepening Understanding of the Universe: Holy fear can lead to a deeper understanding of our place in the universe. Contemplating the vastness of creation and the interconnectedness of all things can foster an appreciation for the complexities of life, contributing to wisdom over time.

4. Access to a Well of Wisdom: Embracing the fear of God provides individuals with access to a well of wisdom

within themselves. This wisdom enables them to make better decisions and live more fulfilling, purposeful lives by understanding their connection to the divine and their role in the world.

5. Guidance and Grace in Life: By fearing God and practicing humility, individuals can navigate life with grace and discernment. This guidance helps them make more informed choices, fostering a sense of purpose and leading to a more fulfilling existence.

Self-Reflection Questions

How can you personally relate to the concept of fearing God as a source of self-awareness and humility?

_____

_____

_____

_____

_____

_____

_____

_____

_____

_____

_____

_____

Have you ever observed instances where constructive fear has encouraged you to reflect on your actions and seek guidance from a higher power? If so, how did this impact your decision-making and wisdom?

_____

_____

_____

_____

_____

_____

_____

_____

_____

_____

_____

_____

Reflecting on your own family or social circle, can you identify instances where the presence or absence of holy fear has had a discernible impact on the trajectory of individuals' lives?

_____

_____

_____

_____

_____

_____

_____

_____

_____

_____

_____

How has contemplating the vastness of creation and the interconnectedness of all things influenced your own appreciation for the complexities of life and your understanding of your place in the universe?

_____

_____

_____

_____

_____

_____

_____

_____

_____

_____

_____

In what ways do you plan to incorporate the concept of fearing God to unlock the well of wisdom within you and live a more fulfilling, purposeful life?

_____

_____

_____

_____

_____

_____

_____

_____

_____

_____

_____

CENTRAL IDEA 5

Fear's Influence on Well-Being.

Key Lessons

1. Deepening Your Connection to the Divine: Developing a profound and transformative relationship with a higher power can be a source of personal growth and spiritual fulfillment. It encourages us to foster a constructive fear of God, creating an environment that nurtures our connection to the divine.

2. Shared Spiritual Foundation in Relationships: This emphasizes how shared faith in the divine can be a powerful foundation for relationships. The author and his wife credit their thriving relationship to their mutual reverence for a higher power, which strengthens their bond as a couple and enriches their individual lives.

3. Self-Reflection and Self-Awareness: Maintaining intimacy with the divine encourages us to reflect on our beliefs, values, and how we express them in our daily lives. This self-awareness helps us better understand our true selves and our place in the world, enabling us to live more authentically and purposefully.

4. Stability and Resilience in Life's Challenges: A strong connection with the divine can provide a sense of stability and solace during life's difficulties. Feeling supported and guided by a higher power equips us to navigate challenging situations with grace and resilience, providing the strength and courage to persevere and grow.

5. Conflict Resolution: This suggests that with a strong connection to the divine, conflicts become more manageable and temporary. Having unwavering faith can anchor us during turbulent times, giving us the inner strength to overcome challenges and grow from our experiences.

Self-Reflection Questions

How do you personally define and experience a deep, intimate relationship with the divine, and how has it transformed your life, if at all?

_____

_____

_____

_____

_____

_____

_____

_____

_____

_____

_____

_____

In your own life, how does fostering a constructive fear of God contribute to creating an environment that nurtures your connection to the divine, and in what ways does this help you grow spiritually?

_____

_____

_____

_____

_____

_____

_____

_____

_____

_____

_____

Reflecting on your own relationships, how has your shared faith in a higher power influenced your ability to cultivate strong communication, mutual respect, and unwavering commitment with your partner or loved ones?

_____

_____

_____

_____

_____

_____

_____

_____

_____

_____

_____

_____

How does maintaining intimacy with the divine impact your examination of personal beliefs and values, and in what ways do you express and manifest these beliefs in your daily life?

_____

_____

_____

_____

_____

_____

_____

_____

_____

_____

_____

_____

In your experience, how has a strong connection with the divine provided you with stability and solace in times of life's challenges, and how does it empower you to navigate difficult situations with grace and resilience?

_____

_____

_____

_____

_____

_____

_____

_____

_____

_____

_____

CENTRAL IDEA 6

Navigating Life's Journey with Principles.

Key Lessons

1. The Fear of God as a Moral Compass: This emphasizes the importance of the fear of God as a foundation for living a purposeful and morally sound life. This fear helps individuals stay grateful for their lives and develop a strong moral compass that guides them toward wisdom, growth, and fulfillment.

2. Respect for Authority and Humility: The story of Justin highlights the significance of respecting authority figures and practicing humility. Justin's initial response to correction from his boss was critical and disrespectful. However, after three months, he realized the need for a proper attitude toward his boss's authority and sought forgiveness.

3. The Power of a Well-Defined Moral Compass: A well-defined moral compass is essential for making difficult decisions and living a life aligned with one's core values and principles. This compass serves as a guide for leading a life of integrity, authenticity, and purpose.

4. Fostering Connection and Unity: A strong moral compass encourages individuals to view the world through the lens of shared humanity. Approaching others with understanding and kindness helps create a sense of connection and unity that transcends differences. This is exemplified by Justin's improved relationship with his boss.

5. Inner Peace and Personal Fulfillment: A strong moral compass not only aids in making wiser decisions but also contributes to personal fulfillment. It helps individuals cultivate inner peace and leads to a more content and meaningful life.

Self-Reflection Questions

How well do you currently maintain a sense of reverence and the fear of God in your life to guide your moral compass?

_____

_____

_____

_____

_____

_____

_____

_____

_____

_____

_____

_____

Have there been instances in your life where you failed to respect authority or lost sight of the importance of treating others with respect? How did you handle those situations, and what did you learn from them?

_____

_____

_____

_____

_____

_____

_____

_____

_____

_____

_____

Do you believe your moral compass is well-defined, and does it effectively guide your decision-making and actions, helping you lead a life of integrity, authenticity, and purpose?

_____

_____

_____

_____

_____

_____

_____

_____

_____

_____

_____

_____

How often do you approach others with understanding and kindness, viewing the world through the lens of our shared humanity? Can you recall specific instances where this approach has improved your relationships or resolved conflicts?

_____

_____

_____

_____

_____

_____

_____

_____

_____

_____

_____

_____

In what ways has your moral compass contributed to your personal growth, wisdom, and inner peace? How do you plan to further strengthen and refine your moral compass in the future?

_____

_____

_____

_____

_____

_____

_____

_____

_____

_____

_____

_____

CENTRAL IDEA 7

Embracing Inner Peace

Key Lessons

1. Fearing God Through Reflection and Stillness: In today's fast-paced and distraction-filled world, it's crucial to find moments of stillness and reflection, which can be grounded in a sense of "holy fear." This practice can help individuals make inner peace their default state of being, whether at home or in the workplace.

2. Work-Life Balance and Professional Benefits: Encouraging employees to incorporate moments of quiet reflection, connecting with a higher power, can empower them to remain calm and focused amid the chaos of corporate life. This, in turn, can lead to improved work-life balance, clarity, and direction in their professional endeavors.

3. Self-Discovery and Personal Growth: The process of introspection, guided by a reverence for the divine, can offer valuable insights into one's true self and how to evolve and thrive. This self-discovery can lead to more authentic and purposeful living, as individuals understand their thoughts, feelings, and actions in the context of their connection to a higher power.

4. Emotional Resilience and Adaptability: Introspection and contemplation increase emotional resilience, equipping individuals to better navigate life's challenges and uncertainties. This deep understanding of one's inner self and relationship with the divine can foster mental fortitude and flexibility, enabling graceful adaptation to changing circumstances.

5. Improved Well-Being and Satisfaction: Engaging in regular moments of reflection and contemplation, with a sense of "holy fear" at the forefront, can significantly impact well-being, mental health, and personal growth. This practice can lead to increased life satisfaction, better mental health, and a sense of closeness to the divine.

Self-Reflection Questions

How do you currently prioritize moments of stillness and reflection in your daily life, and what distractions might be hindering your ability to do so?

_____

_____

_____

_____

_____

_____

_____

_____

_____

_____

_____

In your work environment, how well do you manage to maintain inner peace amidst corporate chaos, and how might connecting with a higher power help you in achieving this calmness?

_____

_____

_____

_____

_____

_____

_____

_____

_____

_____

_____

_____

What steps can you take to create more space for introspection and self-discovery, fostering personal growth and development in your life?

_____

_____

_____

_____

_____

_____

_____

_____

_____

_____

_____

_____

How would you describe your current level of emotional resilience, and in what ways can introspection guided by your reverence for the divine enhance your ability to navigate life's challenges?

_____

_____

_____

_____

_____

_____

_____

_____

_____

_____

_____

_____

Reflect on the role of holy fear and divine connection in your life; how might embracing this concept more fully lead to increased life satisfaction, improved mental health, and a closer relationship with the divine?

_____

_____

_____

_____

_____

_____

_____

_____

_____

_____

_____

Life-Changing Exercises

1. Reflect on Your Fears: Take time to introspect and identify whether you have any destructive fears that are holding you back. Write down these fears and work on transforming them into constructive fears that catalyze positive change in your life.

2. Cultivate Reverence: Develop a practice of reverence for a higher power or the divine. Dedicate time to contemplate the vastness of creation and your place in it. This practice can inspire gratitude, happiness, and inner peace.

3. Embrace Humility: Begin to approach life with humility by recognizing your limitations and being receptive to guidance from a higher power. Practice humility in your interactions with others, and remain open to learning from their perspectives.

4. Strengthen Your Moral Compass: Define your core values and principles and align your actions with them. When faced with difficult decisions, use your moral compass to guide your choices, fostering a life of integrity, authenticity, and purpose.

5. Seek Wisdom: Foster self-awareness through constructive fear by reflecting on your actions and seeking guidance from a higher power. Engage in self-

reflection to gain wisdom that empowers you to navigate life with grace and discernment.

6. Develop a Deep Connection with the Divine: Explore ways to nurture a profound and transformative relationship with a higher power. Cultivate shared faith and spirituality with a loved one to strengthen your connection as a couple and as individuals.

7. Create Space for Stillness and Reflection: Incorporate moments of quiet contemplation into your daily routine. Whether at home or at work, practice reflection in holy fear to make inner peace your default state and find clarity and direction in the chaos of daily life.

8. Strengthen Emotional Resilience: Use your introspective moments to build emotional resilience. Reflect on your inner self and your relationship with the divine to develop the mental fortitude and flexibility needed to adapt to life's challenges with grace and poise.

9. Repair Relationships: If you've had conflicts or misunderstandings with others, reflect on your actions in the context of a constructive fear of God. Use this reflection to find the courage to apologize, make amends, and repair damaged relationships.

10. Live Authentically: Work on living a more authentic and purposeful life by continually aligning your actions with your moral compass and core values. This alignment will empower you to make better decisions and lead a more fulfilling, meaningful existence.

Self-Assessment Questions

Have you consistently applied the concepts and strategies discussed in the workbook to your personal life? Provide specific examples.

_____

_____

_____

_____

_____

_____

_____

_____

_____

_____

_____

_____

What areas of your life have shown the most significant improvement as a result of working through this workbook?

_____

_____

_____

_____

_____

_____

_____

_____

_____

_____

_____

_____

Reflect on your progress in achieving the goals you set at the beginning of the workbook. What have you accomplished, and what remains to be done?

_____

_____

_____

_____

_____

_____

_____

_____

_____

_____

_____

_____

How have you adapted your daily routines and habits to align with the principles outlined in the workbook?

_____

_____

_____

_____

_____

_____

_____

_____

_____

_____

_____

_____

Share examples of how your relationships with others (family, friends, colleagues) have benefited from your personal growth and insights gained from the workbook.

_____

_____

_____

_____

_____

_____

_____

_____

_____

_____

_____

Identify any unexpected discoveries or insights you've had about yourself during this workbook process.

_____

_____

_____

_____

_____

_____

_____

_____

_____

_____

Evaluate your overall satisfaction with your progress and growth throughout the workbook. What would you do differently if you were to start over, and what advice would you offer to someone else embarking on a similar journey?

_____

_____

_____

_____

_____

_____

_____

_____

_____

_____

_____

_____

Made in the USA
Middletown, DE
09 October 2024

62242717R00042